CM007742759

MICHAEL STEIN & THOMAS PFAHL

MINI

The Car, The Cult & The Swinging Beats

IMPRESSUM

COPYRIGHT © 2007 by edel entertainment GmbH, Hamburg/Germany
in cooperation with MINI SCENE INTERNATIONAL / Medieninformations-
dienst (MI).
Please see index for individual photographic copyright.
Please see tracklist credits for music copyrights.

ISBN 978-3-940004-01-7

EDITORIAL DIRECTION
by Astrid Fischer/edel and Jos Bendinelli Negrone/edel

CONCEPT, TEXTS AND PHOTO EDITORIAL
by Michael Stein/MI and Thomas Pfahl/MI

MUSIC SELECTION
by Holger Müssener/HMH and Michael Stein/MI

ART DIRECTION AND GRAPHIC DESIGN
by Wolfgang Seidl, SEIDLDESIGN

TRANSLATION
by Annika Meyer

PRODUCED BY
optimal media production GmbH, Röbel/Germany
Printed and manufactured in Germany

earBOOKS is a division of edel entertainment GmbH
For more information about earBOOKS please visit www.earbooks.net

edel
entertainment GmbH

PREFACE

There are several rather matter-of-fact reference and specialist books containing overly precise treatises about the Mini. However, this MINI earBOOK is different. Images are the main source of information in this book, although the most important and most interesting background information is nevertheless included

in the form of rather brief spoken contributions. Including rare tracks as well as great hits from the years in which the little car became an automobile star for the first time. It is still a star, however, the Mini in its new form has now turned into a cult object for the second time around. In fact, the New Mini has already secured

a substantially large fan club: people for whom their car is much more than just a means of locomotion.
This earBOOK does as much justice to the fun involved in the New Mini as to the passion people feel for the original vehicle no longer produced. Thanks to the large

group of enthusiasts treasuring and cherishing the old Mini and often revive it from pitiful circumstances, the tiny car has indubitably become an immortal classic. That in itself is a remarkable fact, for the Mini – first produced in 1959 and introduced as Austin Seven or Morris Mini-Minor – was originally intended quite simply as a

particularly economical small car. Nobody was likely to imagine the huge mania this vehicle would initiate during the years at the time of its first release. Regardless of whether you prefer the old, the new or indeed like both versions; there is one thing all Mini fans share: their passion for a truly unique vehicle. And

"MINI – The Car, the Cult & The Swinging Beats" is intended as a mirror image of this passion in all its facets.

Michael Stein
Editor-in-chief, Mini Scene International

THE BEGINNING

Tube. (Provides torsion stiffness & front end structure).

Petrol tank (stressed.)

Engine mounting tie

Tube cross member at front on subframe.

Front suspension fitting on tie

unit outside

01

The Mini was never actually conceived as a "cult car". But let's face it, who ever spoke of "cult" back in those days? In any case, the little car from Britain was actually an emergency solution – the Suez crisis of 1956 and the ensuing lack of oil reserves forced the development of economical cars. The British Motor Corporation (BMC) commissioned its head developer, Alec Issigonis, to come up with a suitable vehicle.

Alexander Arnold Constantine Issigonis (to quote his full name) was born on 18 November 1906 and was the son of a Brit with Greek origin. Very early on in his childhood he showed an interest and flair for technology and trained as a mechanical engineer in the UK. But maths wasn't really his passion, he was more of a practitioner. Issigonis designed his own race car and collaborated in various developments in the automobile industry. Despite the adverse post-World War Two conditions, Issigonis and his team built a four-seater prototype – the Morris Minor (1948).

Four seats and an engine – those were the basic requirements of the new project. Issigonis dismissed the tradition of longitudinally mounting the engine at the front coupled with rear-wheel drive as taking up too much space. His idea was in fact much simpler: A transversely-mounted engine could power the front wheels and thus save a lot of space. However, this meant that the gearbox also had to fit in this space. Issigonis drew an idea on a serviette – an action typical of his unconventional style. If the gearbox shared the oil circulation with the engine, it would then be possible to come up with a space-saving design. And that's exactly what the

gifted mechanic did – he managed to keep the drive train compact within the space available. Add four seats, a small boot and hey presto! You've got the basics of a car. But the engine wasn't the only sensation of the Mini: The rubber-cone suspension and 10-inch wheels were also innovations along with the integral body with externally welded seams, all of which helped to simplify and thus reduce the cost of production. The gearbox was mounted on a subframe.

As early as July 1958, Issigonis was testing the Mini on the company's premises together with his boss Leonard Lord. Production of the Mini started in Longbridge and Cowley in May 1959 under the name Austin Seven or Morris Mini-Minor. The small car only sold in small quantities at the beginning, but by 1962 more

than 200,000 vehicles were leaving the showrooms. The rallying success of the Mini boosted both sales as well as the car's image, with more and more (pseudo-)celebrities buying it on account of its attractiveness. Once this had happened, nothing stood in the way of the Mini's success. Racing drivers, actors, even members of the British royal family bought a Mini. Along with its success came global recognition, which led to the knighting of Issigonis on 22 July 1969 by Queen Elizabeth II. This was however the end of the revolutions: the Mini series was constantly added to with new models, the main changes of which were limited to the addition of modern technology rather than aesthetic modifications. The concept of the transversely-mounted front engine is still used in today's medium-sized cars.

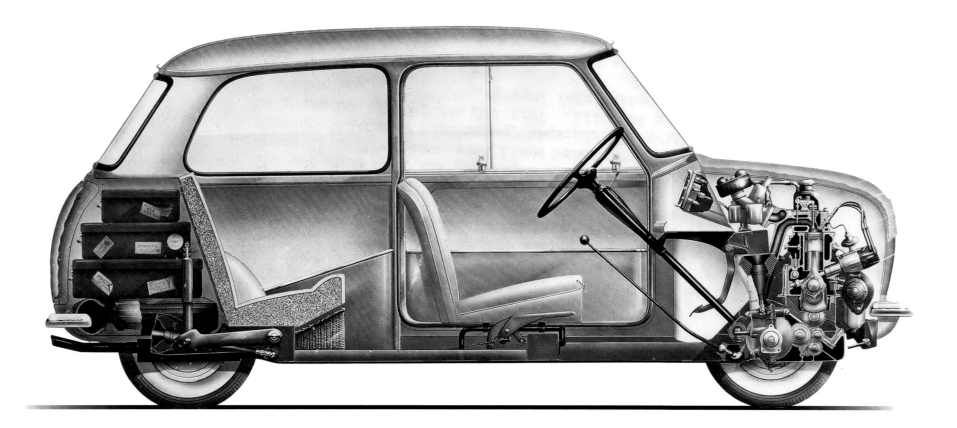

AUSTIN mini DE LUXE SALOON

See, now, the most fascinating and widely acclaimed version of the Mini. Pert and smart in appearance, the Austin Mini De Luxe Saloon is fully equipped with every motoring refinement. Among the additional items of exterior equipment included on the De Luxe Saloon are wheel embellishers, bumper overriders supplemented by tubular extensions, bright finishers to windscreen and backlight, and stainless surrounds to the lower panel sills and opening rear windows.

A range of exciting colours is available on all Austin Minis and there is an eye-catching trim chosen to complete each colour scheme. Driving equipment is second to none. Take a trip through the darkness and see how the double-dip headlamps and flashing direction indicators provide the necessary confidence for comfortable night driving. You will find also that in fair weather or foul, the screen can be kept perfectly clean because in addition to the twin wiper blades, windscreen washers are fitted to all Austin Mini Saloons.

Inside and out there are many more fascinating and exclusively designed features to commend this revolutionary Austin Mini — a worthy successor to the famous line of small cars which started as a dream of the late Lord Austin in 1921.

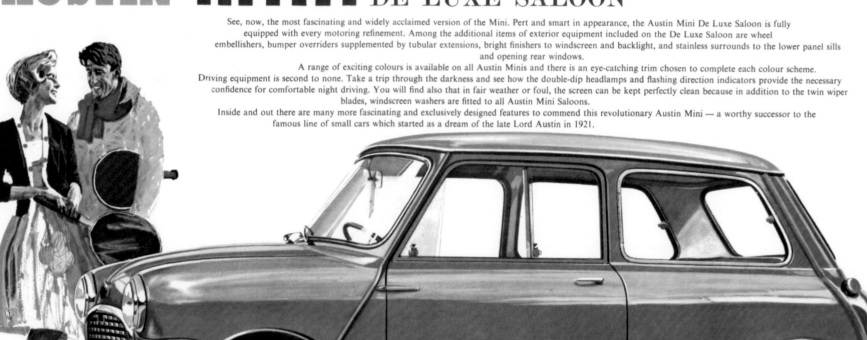

AUSTIN Incredible **min**

★ Comb
★ Safety
★ Two-le
★ Greate

...now with Hyd

aloon....

...ition/starter switch.

...ors and interior mirror.

...hoe brakes at front.

...e capacity gearbox.

...astic suspension!

JCG351E

FROM MINI TO MINI COOPER

02

Although Sir Alec Issigonis immediately took to racing with his **first car**, the Mini was not originally designed as a sports car. The Mini's introduction to the racing scene was the result of Issigonis' long-standing friendship with John Cooper, who was born on 17 July 1923.

Issigonis valued Cooper's opinion in his capacity as a passionate racing driver and car designer. Cooper actually used several Morris engines in his cars. In 1946 Cooper's father founded the Cooper Car Company, which went on to produce many powerful and successful racing cars. To a certain extent John Cooper was involved in the Mini's development right from the beginning. He knew the car from top to bottom and recognised its major potential. He saw a genuine competitor for the Lotus Elite, which dominated motorsport at that time.

However, Issigonis didn't see the Mini as a sports car. Despite this fact, BMC boss George Harriman soon came up with the idea of bringing out a little "GT", the result of which was a small production run in 1960/1961. As the engine in this category was not allowed to exceed 1,000 cc, Cooper increased the stroke while reducing the bore correspondingly. This produced an engine size of 997 cc. Thanks to improved compression, larger valves and a dual carburettor, the small engine was able to churn out 55 bhp. Incidentally, these engines were also used in the Cooper Formula Junior race cars.

In September 1961 Issigonis and Cooper pushed the idea even further: The Cooper S was launched on the market with a 1071 cc engine and 70 bhp to boot. The road-going Cooper also acquired a big brother in the form of a rally version, with six works cars entering the Monte Carlo rally in 1960. When the range of models

was reworked in 1967, the Cooper was temporarily removed from the range and replaced by the 1275 GT. Despite this move, dedicated Mini buyers could still choose from various Cooper tuning kits. The first official Cooper after that time did not appear until 1990, at which time Rover was in charge of the Mini range. Along with the other Mini models, the Cooper was also fitted with a 1 litre carburettor engine until 1992, at which time stricter exhaust gas regulations meant that the engine had to be replaced by the 1275 engine with fuel injection.

Of course John Cooper wasn't just involved in developing fast Minis – he was also one of the pioneers of the mid-engine design used in the Formula 1 cars that helped Jack Brabham to become World Champion. His name also lives on in the New Mini range. The new Cooper (and later the Cooper S) was presented in 2001. The John

Cooper Works range continues to offer Mini drivers various options to refine and customise their car. Options range from performance boosts to more than 200 bhp through to optical refinement right up to the special model "JCW GP".

Unfortunately John Cooper was not able to experience the new generation of "his" car – he died on 24 December 2000. His son Mike Cooper has majestically taken up where his father left off, meaning that the family name will continue to be associated with the Mini in years to come...

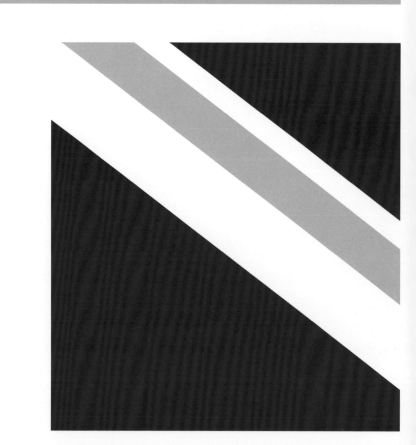

MUCH MORE THAN A CAR

03

The Mini is on the verge of celebrating fifty years since it was first presented. At that time no-one suspected the huge popularity that the little car from Longbridge would gather and enjoy over the years. The car's backdrop was in fact somewhat more sobering, as it was actually developed as a small family car during periods of economic difficulty. However, over the course of time its unique design, fascinating technical concept and sporting success has bestowed the Mini with absolute cult status. And that's not all. The new interpretation of the Mini, which has been available since production of the old Mini was halted in 2000, achieved immediate success and became an instant, modern-day lifestyle icon.

Enthusiasm for the Mini can be seen in the form of its fans and enthusiasts who pursue their love of the car, both old and new, in a multitude of different ways. Whether it's restoring and maintaining a classic, tuning and motorsport, or simply the urge to be part of a global community – Mini clubs, not just in Great Britain but all over the world, were founded many years ago and have grown from strength to strength. There are also special race meetings and rallies, some

of which attract huge crowds and enthusiasts. Such events include the international meetings of Mini Classic fans in various locations. These are complemented by events such as "Strahlung pur" (Pure Exuberance), "Hamburg Mini Days" and the "Braunschweiger Mini Tage" (Braunschweig Mini Days) in Germany, "Mini Mania" in the UK, "Mini Mucchio" in Italy or "Mini takes the States" in the USA. Particularly worthy of mention is the fact that the Mini community is given special support by private and works-independent entities as well as BMW. So far, the biggest event of this kind is "Mini United" which premiered in Misano, Italy, in 2005. On this first occasion, approximately 6000 Mini fans from 40 countries travelled to the Adriatic coast with more than 4000 cars. A further meeting took place in June 2007 with the North Sea providing the backdrop for the mega event. The organisers of the event at the Dutch "Circuit Park" in Zandvoort recorded 8000 visitors – a considerable increase on the first meeting which had already been a remarkable success. We can therefore look forward with anticipation to the further development of "Mini United"...

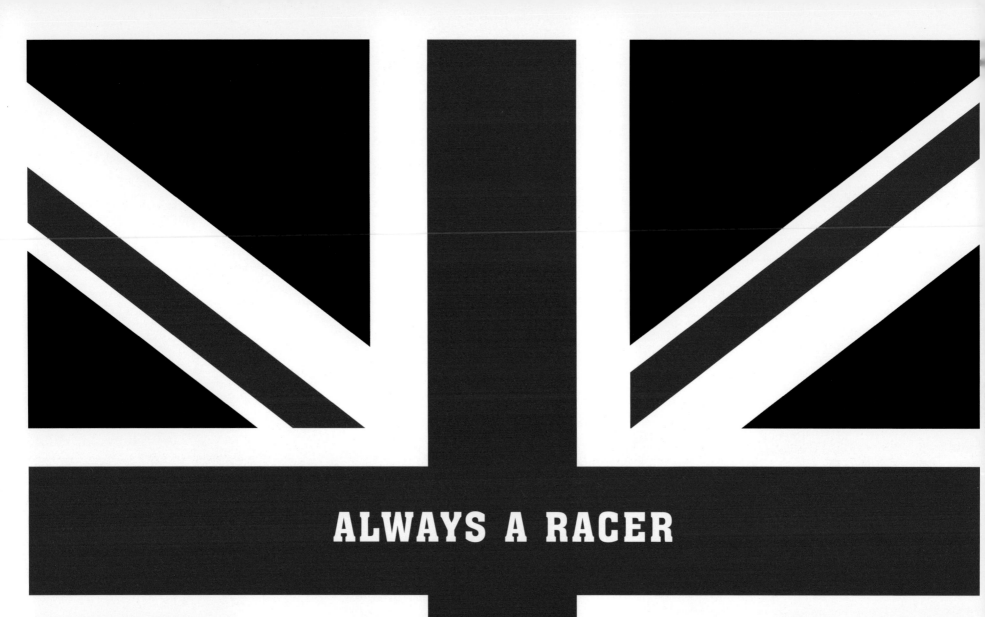

ALWAYS A RACER

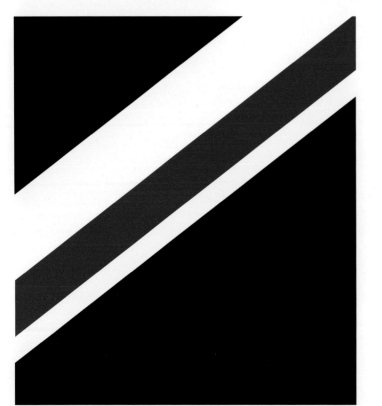

ORX
707F 1968 185 1968 RALLYE MONTE-CARLO

04

There's no doubt about it – when the Mini premiered in 1959 it was a sensation. And as car manufacturers like to prove their expertise in the motorsport scene, the British Motor Company (BMC) sent the Mini out onto the race track. Six months after the market launch, six works cars took part in the Monte Carlo rally. These cars were accompanied at the start of the race by six other private Minis. The Riley/Jones team achieved the highest Mini ranking: a sobering 23rd place.

In 1961 none of the three works cars reached the finish. Following this disappointment, the mechanics at BMC tinkered away on the Minis behind the scenes. In 1962 the Minis were back at the Monte Carlo rally. The Finn Rauno Aaltonen was called upon to put things right for the BMC. However, the car somersaulted before burning out. The remaining works Minis finished the race in 26th and 77th place. BMC also monitored the rest of the field: The private driver Timo Mäkinen performed quite well in his Cooper,

and the Irishman Patrick Hopkirk was followed with suspicion in his Sunbeam Rapier. Just one year later Hopkirk was at the wheel of one of the works Minis, finishing up second in the class behind team colleague Aaltonen, with the Finn finishing up third overall and the Irishman sixth. In doing so they attracted the attention of the rallying world: Two little cars were running rings around the "big boys"!

The breakthrough came in 1964: six works and 24 private Minis lined up alongside the supposedly strong competition. The rest is written in the history books: Paddy Hopkirk won the Monte Carlo rally! The next Mini driver, Timo Mäkinen, came in fourth with Aaltonen finishing up seventh overall. The results sent a wave through the world of motorsport!

Success was now obligatory: The 1965 Monte Carlo rally and the 52nd event were arguably the hardest test on both man and machine. The ice and snow separated the men from the boys with

just 35 of the 237 cars that started the race reaching the finish! Three Minis were among the few cars that made it to the end, one of which was driven by Timo Mäkinen and Christobel Carlisle who won the race overall!

In 1966 a hotly-contested decision made by the Federation Internationale de l'Automobile in Paris denied the British cars their Monte Carlo hat trick. Mäkinen, Aaltonen and Hopkirk left the rest of the field in their wake. But a technical inspection showed that the extra headlamps mounted in front of the radiator didn't meet the Federation's requirements.

In 1968, BMC boss Lord Stokes decided to dissolve the motorsport division, but not before the Mini gang had one last go at climbing the Col de Turini. Aaltonen, Fall and Hopkirk finished third, fourth and fifth respectively, meaning that the Mini bowed out from the Monte Carlo rally in true style. However, this did not mean the end of the Mini and motorsport – the "little Brit" still appears at classic car races such as the British Car Trophy in Germany, at rallies and regularity tests. Countless private teams still highly rate the driving qualities of the classic Mini.

The New Mini is also on its way to becoming a popular race car – The John Cooper Challenge was initiated by Mike Cooper and launched in 2002 with seasoned drivers lining up against hot-blooded youngsters. National championships (also grouped under the name "Mini Challenge") were established as a result of the growing popularity of the event. A world final was held for the first time in Misano in 2005, with the Belgian Maxime Martin taking the chequered flag.

Famous star guests appear time and again to race in one of the 200 bhp Minis. The drivers enjoy the cart-like handling of the JCW Cooper S, while the spectators look forward to watching the exciting battles out on the race track involving up to forty similar cars. The Mini and motorsport – a marriage made in heaven!

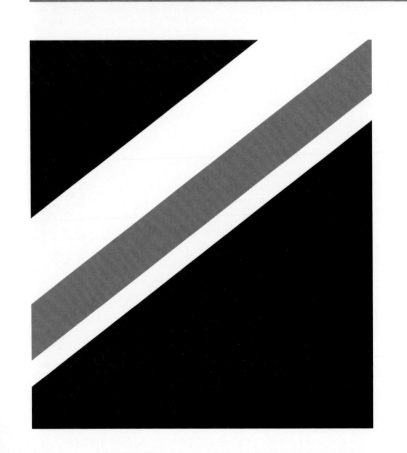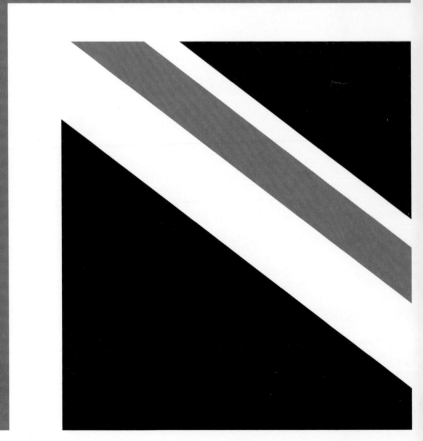

VARIETIES AND FANTASIES

05

The Mini has stimulated people's imaginations ever since its first appearance, and this phenomenon stretches beyond the imaginations of fans who tinker with their own Mini from time to time. Designers and engineers alike also yearn to turn their hand to the little car. Their main aim in modifying the "little Brit" over the years was to attract differing and new customer groups. People unfamiliar with the Mini range may not even recognise certain models as being a modification of the original. The most obvious example of this was the Moke, which was originally earmarked as a military vehicle. With this particular "pack horse", initial tests carried out at the start

even involved two engines! A 950 cc engine was mounted at the front with an 850 cc production engine at the back with the aim of turning the vehicle based on the Mini Countryman into a 4x4 machine suitable for off-road use. However, the first prototype tests quickly showed that the Moke was no match for a Jeep or Land Rover. The main problems included cooling and synchronisation of the two engines. Tests were then carried out using two Austin 1100 engines before the "Twin Mini" concept was finally banned to history. Numerous other concepts followed before the Moke was finally released on the civilian market as a front-wheel-drive leisure vehicle

powered by an 850 cc engine, enough for a trip to the countryside or the beach. The somewhat well-to-do target group considered the Moke a real trend-setting vehicle.

But most other Mini variants tended not to vary as wildly from the original as the Moke. The pick-up models that now enjoy cult status show their roots much more clearly, while the Clubmans stand out on account of their front end, which barely resembles a Mini. The noble Wolseleys, the smart Cabrio, the Countryman, the Mini Van or Estate, both of which were designed as transporters – whichever concoction of the Mini you take, variety is always the central role at the heart of it all. Models that didn't roll off the production line are also highly sought after among external providers. Just look at the sporty Midas (based on the Mini) or the Nomad, the creation of a British manufacturer made to look like a Land Rover. Anything that the imagination and fantasy of enthusiastic mechanics and hardened Mini enthusiasts conjures up is often happily made reality. The ideas that people come up with range from a Big Foot to fun cars right through to stretch limousines.

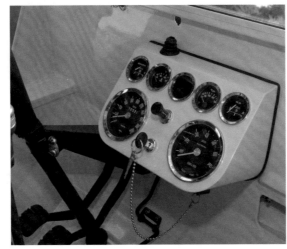

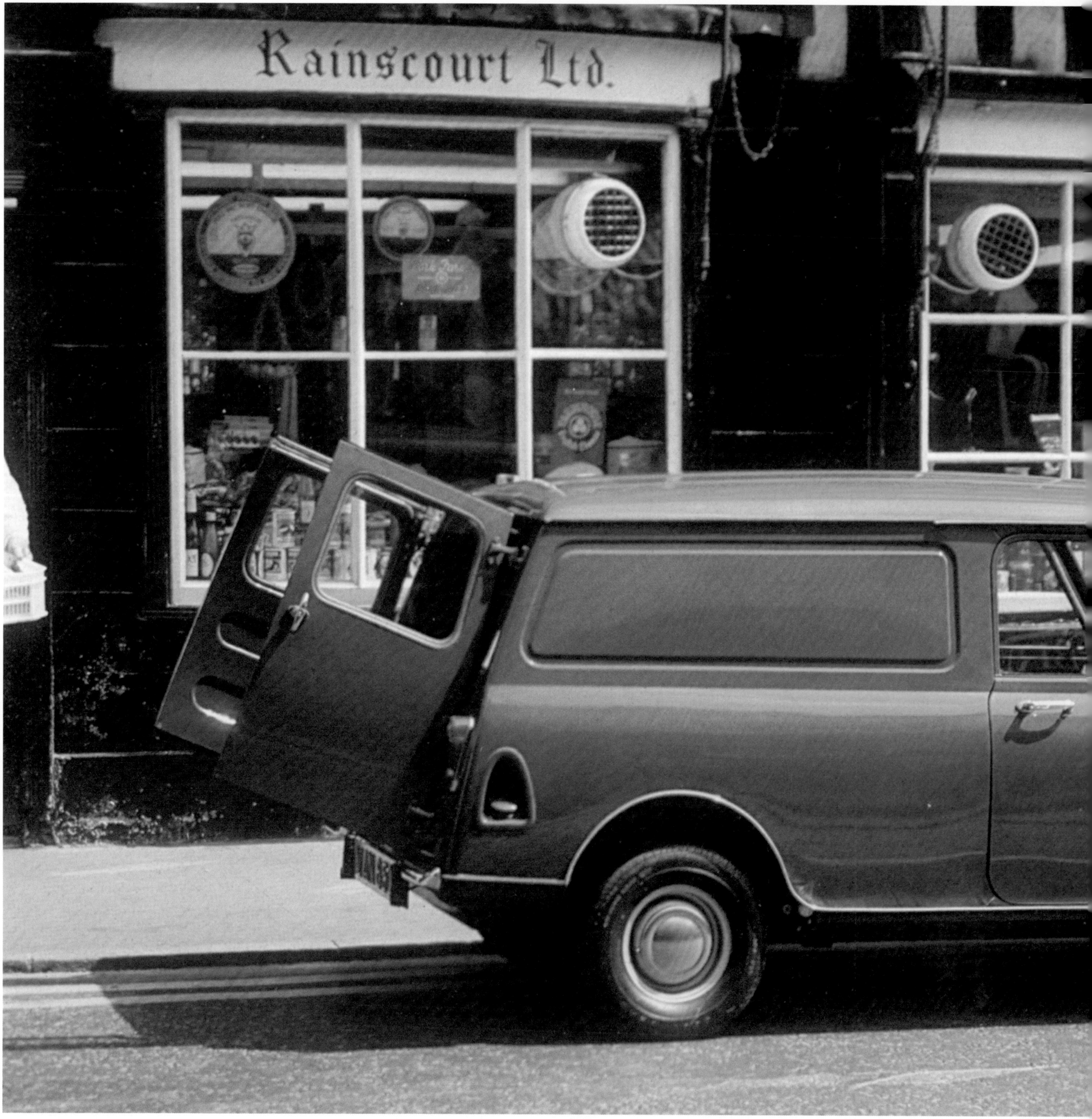
Rainscourt Ltd.

AUSTIN
850 *Countryman*

BUSINESS BEFORE PLEASURE...

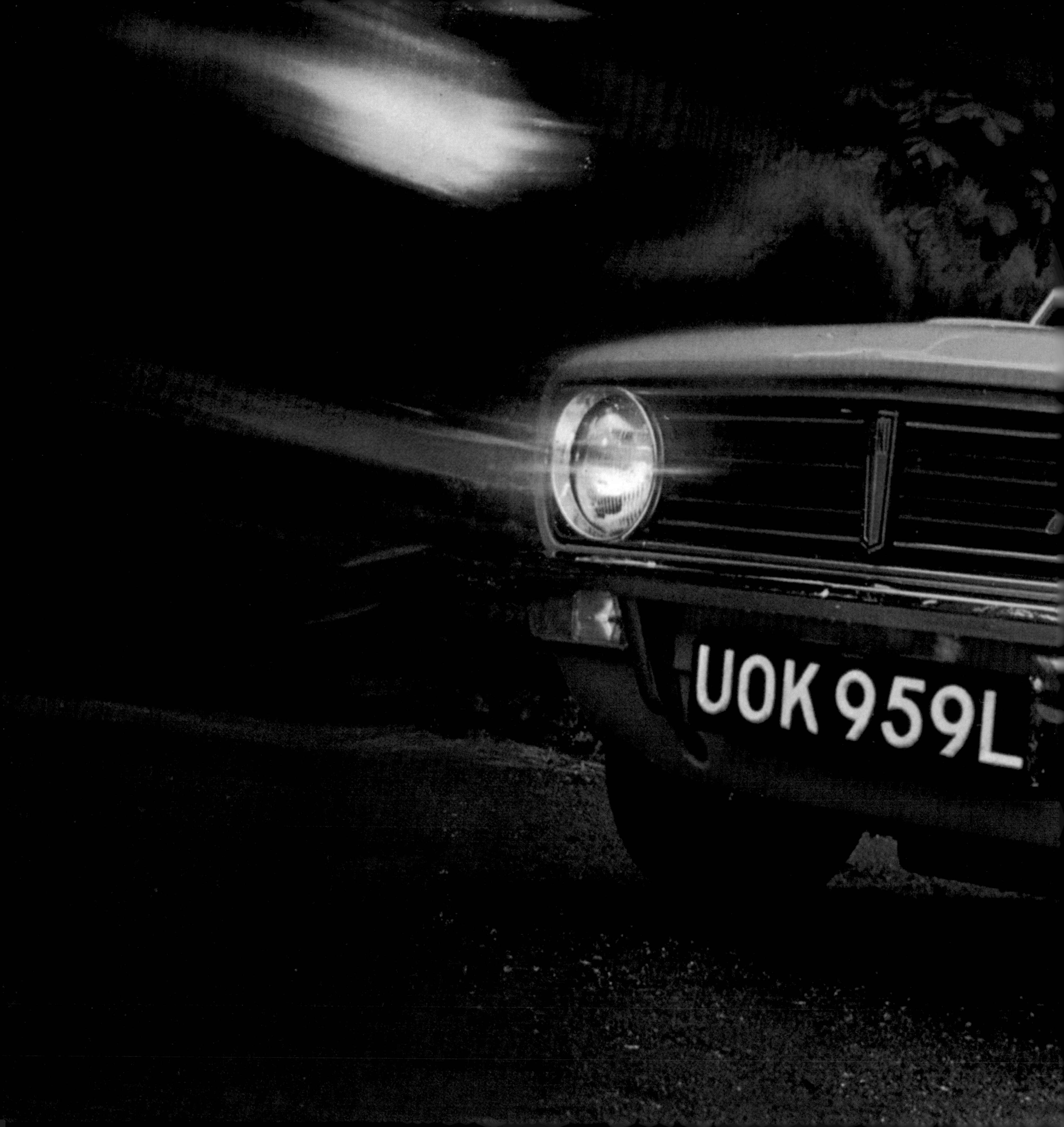
UOK 959L

THE LEGEND LIVES!

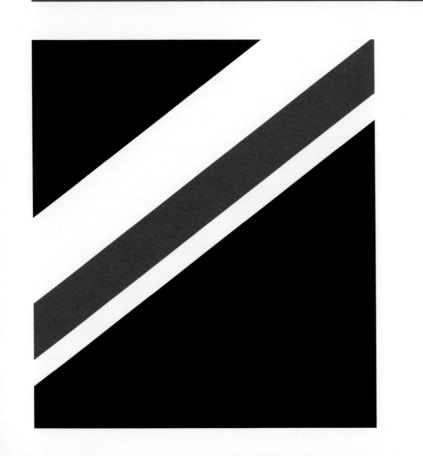
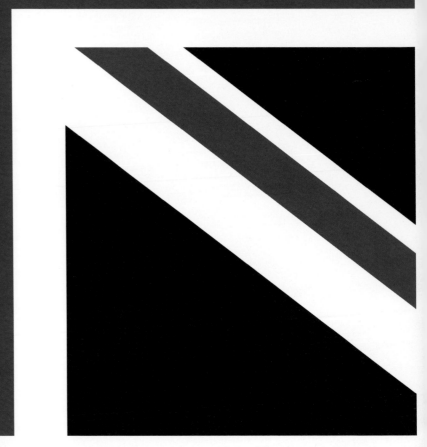

06

For countless owners, the Mini is without doubt more than just a vehicle for getting from A to B. But despite the emotions connected with the car, the little Brit was still subject to purely rational decisions. Having been manufactured almost without change for more than four decades, production of the familiar and well-loved Mini was halted in 2000. Its obsolescence was immediately followed up by the market launch of a new interpretation from BMW.

The development of the Mini for the new millennium wasn't just harking back to the good old days of its predecessor. No, no – the New Mini, presented in Paris in September 2000, was an evolution of the original. The similarities the New Mini shares with its predecessor were only apparent in name and basic shape. Having said that, as was the case with the classic Mini built in the UK, the New Mini was initially only available in the basic version, One, and the sporty version, Cooper. Both models were powered with a four-cylinder, 1.6 litre engine with 90 bhp and 115 bhp respectively. These models were to be quickly added to by other engines and models, including a cabriolet. In 2006 a new version of the New Mini was launched, with BMW heralding a change of New Mini generation at the end of the year. A more obvious sign that the classic Mini's successor has overcome all of the gloomy predictions bestowed upon it is simply not possible.

The MkII continued the evolution course of the MkI, embodied in a way that only a Mini can. As expected, external modifications

were approached with a very fine paintbrush. At first glance the New Mini MkII doesn't actually look particularly "new", despite the fact that every single body part was redesigned. However, upon closer examination it is possible to see certain changes to the optics: The slightly raised bonnet and bonnet scoop of the MkII comes across somewhat beefier than its predecessor, while the rear end has seen the majority of the style changes, with the overall look harking back to the Mini's long-standing sporting roots. The interior has also been completely redesigned, and now has a striking and large centrally-mounted speedo. In terms of technology, the latest "new" model has earned its name in the true sense of the word. The main change here is the introduction of two new engines. Prior to saying goodbye to the MkI in 2007, and in order to demonstrate the new range of models, the MkII Cooper and Cooper S were presented to the public. The 175 bhp 1.6 litre engine of the Cooper S is boosted with a twin-scroll turbo while the Cooper comes with a 120 bhp normally-aspirated BMW Valvetronic engine. Also not to be forgotten is the fact that the not-so-small Mini has grown a further six centimetres when compared with its older brother.

Despite this statistic, the New Mini has won over the hearts of a large fan group, which is growing all the time. It goes without saying that the current Mini has joined its predecessor in proving that it has what it takes to emotionally reach out to people and convince them of its charm. There's no doubt about it: The legend lives!

NEVER BEFORE HAS SO MUCH BEEN PUT INTO SO LITTLE FOR SO FEW.

THE LATEST STEP

07

In car manufacturing, each model series thrives on change - this is equally true for the New Mini as for its predecessors. There were always new variations and it was only a question of time until a new estate car would wheel into the dealers' showrooms. However, it is a long way from the first design sketch to a production model. At the 2005/2006 car exhibitions, the design team around Gerd Hildebrand presented four examples of what a future „Traveller" - as the former estate was called - might look like.

The joy to travel was the focus of the IAA in Frankfurt. When opening the rear doors, a flexible pull-out cargo box becomes visible. White leather, chrome and aluminium invite you to take a seat and drive off. Note the little gimmick: the cup-holders have been installed directly in front of the vent openings. The air conditioning thus keeps the drinks cool in the summer whilst the heating will keep tea or coffee warm in winter.

„Go British" was the theme in Tokyo. The iridescent „Satellite Silver" has been accentuated with elements of green and brass as a reminder of the classic „British Racing Green" of English race cars. The brass accessories mirror the flair of London gentlemen's clubs. Integrated picnic boxes replace the side windows. A removable roof panel can be used as a table if need be and the Sports Utility Box accommodates whatever else makes for a successful summer afternoon, e.g. the cricket or tennis gear.

„Go Sports!" was the motto in Detroit where the serialisation of the Traveller was announced. It was a rough-and-ready concept akin to a typically American SUV. You can pack your sports gear into the

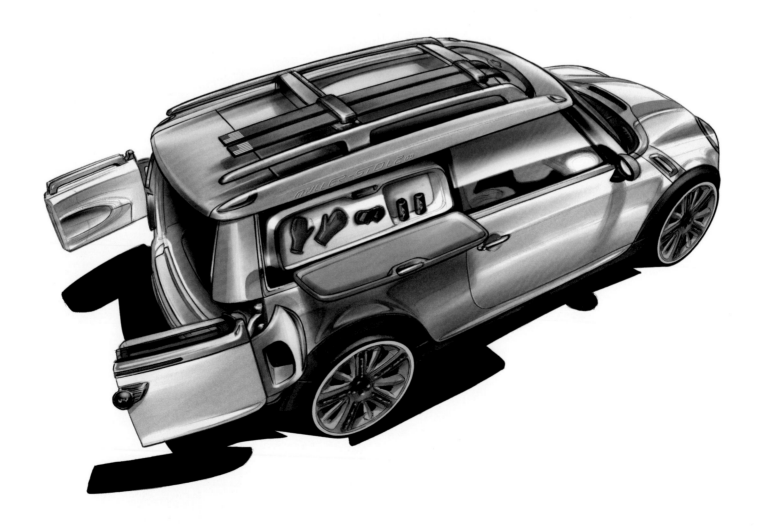

demountable loading box at home and mount it quickly before you leave. You can even take a surfboard thanks to the hatch above the tailgates. The crossbeams on the roof railing of the Detroit concept car can be adjusted. If all else fails, you can mount a roof box to the Mini. Red and blue elements or the stripes on the bonnet are a salute to the host country's „stars & stripes".

The fourth example was presented at Mini 2006 in Geneva. We were reminded of the legendary victory at the 1964 Monte Carlo Rally. The Sports Utility Box has been converted into a toolbox and everything the driver and co-driver might need en-route has its place in it whilst the cargo box provides loading space for spare parts. A prominent feature of rally cars is the spare wheel in easy reach. The Geneva concept car provides a recess in the roof from which the

fifth wheel can be released with two bow-shaped handles. The two additional headlamps in the grill are „typical rally". This concept had to be in red-and-white for obvious reasons - since the 24th of January 1964, if not before, this colour combination has been a cult amongst mini-drivers.

The four different studies were used to test the response from the audience. Which gimmick was to be kept and what was dispensable? The serial model, the Clubman, was finally presented at the International Motor Show, IAA, in Frankfurt in 2007. The distinctive, wide-opening tailgates are still there and the estate car could thus become a van. It would certainly be a welcome and popular feature for courier companies and handicraft businesses…

DAVID BEASLEY 2005

MINI MUSIC – THE BEAT GOES ON...

08

The idea of an earBOOK with a Mini theme might have seemed rather unusual, however, it was, in fact, an obvious one. Nothing could have better complemented our portfolio of photos and archive material than a collection of musical pieces from the years when the Mini became a true cult object almost in spite of itself, having originally been devised as a purely rational design concept for a small car. The collection of four CDs with more than 40 tracks is, as it were, as much the soundtrack of a success story as well as, quite simply, music enhancing the fun factor of the Mini.

This kind of compilation inevitably had to be as multi-faceted as the Mini had proved to be only a short time after its introduction into the market. That is why the music includes everything from the unpolished beats of the early days of the little car to a number of pop tracks and colourful glam rock – in short, music that has accompanied the Mini on its journey to automobile stardom.

There is no question about it: Mini and music have always belonged together. Not least in that many artistes drive or have driven it themselves or have been inspired through it. Cliff Richard

had a Mini, and each one of the Beatles. Tragically, Marc Bolan of T. Rex died after a road accident in a Clubman 1275 GT. Allegedly, the worldwide hit "Keep On Running" occurred to Spencer Davis during a nocturnal overland drive in a Mini that was threatening to run out of fuel. David Bowie was amongst the celebrities that, in an event on the occasion of the 40 year jubilee of the Mini in 1999, were invited to design their own personal variant. The result: a completely chrome-plated exemplar! On the manufacturer side, from the beginning Mini and music were always being brought together, a facet also being continued under its new banner. For example, whereas at that time a Walkman and a Soul and Chart-Hits cassette lay in the special edition model "Red Hot" on its purchase, in 2006 Boy George was engaged as DJ for the Mini's Urban Style Tour. And recently, with "Def Mini Records", a label was set up that presented bands such as "The Disc Brakes", "Runflat" or "N'Cap". Sure, it's only a promotional gimmick – but, in whatever way Mini and music come together, there is no doubt: The Beat goes on…

SMOOTH ON THE STREETS

Jet Black

THE NEW LIMITED EDITION MINI!

FREE ORIGINAL SOUL AND

CHART HITS CASSETTE!

SUPER SONY WALKMAN

OFFER!

THE AUTHORS

Michael Stein, born in 1959, completed an additional course as Technical Editor upon graduating from the Ruhruniversität Bochum/Germany. His enthusiasm for extraordinary vehicles brought him to journalism, a career he started by working for the German edition of the Swedish journal "Wheels". Meanwhile, Michael Stein has been working for several renowned motorists' magazines published by the Vestische Mediengruppe Welke (Herten/Germany) for almost 15 years, and became a first-rate expert of the European scene of car enthusiasts and tuning fans during this time. Similarly, he frequents most relevant international trade fairs or accepts invitations for test drives and product presentations extended on the part of the vehicle and accessories industry. As the editor-in-chief of MINI SCENE INTERNATIONAL and because of his regular journalistic contributions on music, Michael Stein has all the professional expertise needed for the topics covered In this earBOOK.

Thomas Pfahl, born in 1973, is a man who lives for cars with all his heart and soul. He grew up near that legendary German race course, the Nürburgring; and from his earliest childhood displayed genuine enthusiasm for anything on four wheels. Motorsport, both race course events and rallies, always played an important role for him. Quite appropriately, after his school-leaving exams, he completed an apprenticeship as a car mechanic. In 1997, Thomas Pfahl decided to add the camera to his existing tools such as the spanner: following a traineeship in the editing team of a daily paper, he did another period of training with the Vestische Mediengruppe Welke. Henceforth, he contributed to several journals. Every day, he throws some light onto many vehicles of all kinds – lovingly finished or restored by their owners – in both text and images, attends car events, test drives newly developed vehicles or discusses them with designers and designing engineers. Thomas Pfahl has been associated with MINI SCENE INTERNATIONAL as desk editor since its very first edition, published in September 2005.

VORWORT

Eher nüchtern gehaltene Fach- und Sachbücher mit übermäßig detaillierten Abhandlungen zum Thema Mini gibt es etliche. Doch das earBOOK „MINI – The Car, The Cult & The Swinging Beats" ist anders. Ohne darauf zu verzichten, die wichtigsten und interessantesten Hintergrundinformationen anhand einzelner eher knapp gehaltener Wortbeiträge zu liefern, lässt dieses Buch hauptsächlich Bilder sprechen. Darüber hinaus machen vier CDs aus dem Band ein earBOOK mit einer hochkarätigen Musikkollektion. Enthalten sind sowohl rare Tracks als auch große Hits aus den Jahren, in denen der Winzling zum automobilen Star avancierte. Was er fraglos immer noch ist, wobei der Mini in Form seiner Neuauflage bereits das zweite Mal zum Kultobjekt mutierte. Denn dem New Mini gehört längst eine beachtlich große Anhängerschaft: Menschen, denen ihr Auto weitaus mehr bedeutet, als ein Fortbewegungsmittel zu sein.

Dem Spaß am New Mini wird dieses earBOOK ebenso gerecht wie der Leidenschaft für das nicht mehr gebaute ursprüngliche Fahrzeug. Dank der großen Zahl von Enthusiasten, die den alten Mini hegen und pflegen, ja oft aus erbarmungswürdiger Substanz wieder auferstehen lassen, ist das winzige Auto fraglos zu einem unsterblichen Klassiker geworden. Ein äußerst bemerkenswerter Umstand, schließlich sollte der 1959 erstmalig produzierte Mini – zunächst als Austin Seven oder Morris Mini-Minor eingeführt – von seinem Grundgedanken her ja einfach nur ein besonders wirtschaftlicher Kleinstwagen sein. Für welch gewaltige Manie er im Laufe der Jahre sorgen würde, konnte damals wohl niemand vorausahnen.

Ganz egal, ob man nun besonders an der alten, der neuen oder auch an beiden Varianten Gefallen findet, eines haben alle Fans des Mini gemeinsam: die Begeisterung für ein wirklich einzigartiges Fahrzeug. Und ein Spiegelbild eben dieser Begeisterung in all ihren Facetten soll „MINI – The Car, The Cult & The Swinging Beats" sein.

Michael Stein
Chefredakteur, Mini Scene International

1. THE BEGINNING

Eigentlich war der Mini gar nicht als „Kult-Auto" gedacht. Okay, wer sprach damals überhaupt schon von „Kult"? Wie auch immer - der britische Kleinwagen wurde eigentlich aus der Not heraus geboren. Die Suez-Krise 1956 und die damit einhergehende Öl-Knappheit machten sparsame Autos notwendig. BMC beauftragte seinen Chef-Entwickler Alec Issigonis, ein entsprechendes Fahrzeug zu konstruieren.

Alexander Arnold Constantine Issigonis – so der vollständige Name – wurde am 18.11.1906 als Sohn eines Briten griechischer Herkunft geboren. Schon seit frühester Kindheit begeisterte er sich für Technik, machte in England eine Ausbildung zum Maschinenbauer. Doch Mathematik war nicht so sein Ding, er war eher der Praktiker. Issigonis konstruierte einen eigenen Rennwagen und wirkte an diversen Entwicklungen in der Automobilbranche mit. Sein Team hatte unter den widrigen Umständen nach dem zweiten Weltkrieg einen viersitzigen Prototypen auf die Räder gestellt – den Morris Minor (1948).

Vier Sitze und ein Motor - das waren auch die Grundbedingungen des neuen Projekts. Issigonis hielt die damals übliche Bauweise mit einem längs eingebauten Frontmotor und Heckantrieb für zu platzaufwändig. Eigentlich war die Idee ziemlich simpel: ein quer montiertes Triebwerk könnte die Vorderräder antreiben und würde so viel Platz sparen. Allerdings musste das Getriebe auch noch untergebracht werden. Issigonis skizzierte seine Idee auf einer Serviette – das war typisch für seine unkonventionelle Art. Wenn sich das Getriebe den Ölkreislauf mit dem Motor teilte, wäre eine entsprechend platzsparende Bauweise realisierbar. Und in der Tat gelang es dem begnadeten Tüftler, den Antriebsstrang äußerst kompakt zu halten. Dazu noch vier Sitzplätze, ein kleiner Kofferraum und fertig war das Minimum an Auto. Doch der Motor war nicht die einzige Sensation: Gummifederung und 10-Zoll-Räder gehörten ebenso zu den Neuerungen wie die selbsttragende Karosserie mit den äußeren Schweißnähten – das vereinfachte und verbilligte somit die Produktion. Der Antrieb wurde auf einem Hilfsrahmen montiert. Bereits im Juli 1958 kurvte Issigonis mit seinem Chef Leonard Lord über das Werksgelände. Im Mai 1959 lief die Produktion des Mini – damals hieß er noch Austin Seven oder Morris Mini-Minor - in Longbridge und Cowley an. Zunächst wurde das kleine Auto nur schleppend angenommen, doch schon 1962 lieferte man erstmals über 200.000 Fahrzeuge aus. Die Rallye-Erfolge kurbelten Verkauf und Image an, als dann auch immer mehr (Pseudo-)Promis weltweit es schick fanden, sich im Mini zu zeigen, war die Erfolgsstory nicht mehr aufzuhalten. Rennfahrer, Schauspieler, sogar Mitglieder des britischen Königshauses legten sich einen Mini zu. Seine Erfolge brachten ihm weltweite Anerkennung und Issigonis am 22. Juli 1969 den Ritterschlag durch die Königin von England. Weitere Revolutionen gab es an diesem Auto nicht mehr: die Mini-Baureihe wurde dennoch immer wieder um neue Varianten erweitert, die moderne Technik hielt trotz des nach wie vor nostalgischen Äußeren Einzug. Das Konzept des quer eingebauten Frontmotors wird heute noch sogar bis in die Mittelklasse verwendet.

2. FROM MINI TO MINI COOPER

Obwohl Sir Alec Issigonis gleich mit seinem ersten Auto auf die Rennstrecke ging, war der Mini ursprünglich nicht als Motorsportler konzipiert. Die langjährige Freundschaft zum am 17. Juli 1923 geborenen John Cooper war es vielmehr, die den Kleinwagen zum Rasen brachte.

Issigonis schätzte die Meinung des leidenschaftlichen Rennfahrers und Automobil-Konstrukteurs, der im übrigen viele seiner Motoren von Morris bezog. 1946 hatte dessen Vater die Cooper Car Company gegründet, in der viele schlagkräftige Rennwagen entstanden waren. John Cooper war von Beginn an in gewisser Weise in die Entwicklung des Mini involviert, er kannte das Auto von der Pike auf und erkannte sein beachtliches Potential. Er sah in ihm einen echten Wettbewerber für den damals dominierenden Lotus Elite.

Doch für Issigonis war der Mini kein Sportwagen. BMC-Chef George Harriman allerdings fand schnell Gefallen an der Idee, einen kleinen „GT" herauszubringen. 1960/61 entstand eine erste Kleinserie. Da der Hubraum in dieser Klasse nicht größer als 1000 ccm sein durfte, erhöhte Cooper den Hub, während er die Bohrung entsprechend verringerte. Es ergab sich ein Hubraum von 997 ccm. Mit höherer Verdichtung, größeren Ventilen und dem Doppelvergaser erzeugte der kleine Motor 55 PS. Diese Motoren kamen übrigens auch in den Formel-Junior-Rennwagen Coopers zum Einsatz.

Im September 1961 setzten Issigonis und Cooper noch einen drauf: der Cooper S kam auf den Markt – mit 1071 ccm und 70 PS. Parallel zur Entwicklung der Straßen-Cooper entstand auch gleich eine Rallye-Version: schon 1960 starteten sechs Werkswagen zur Rallye Monte Carlo.

Als die Modellpalette 1967 überarbeitet wurde, nahm man den Cooper 1967 vorläufig aus dem Programm und ersetzte ihn durch den 1275 GT. Trotzdem hatten engagierte Mini-Käufer nach wie vor die Wahl zwischen verschiedenen Cooper-Tuning-Kits. Erst 1990, Rover war mittlerweile für die Mini-Baureihe verantwortlich, gab es wieder einen offiziellen Cooper. Bis 1992 wurde er auch mit der 1-Liter-Vergasermaschine ausgestattet, aufgrund der verschärften Abgas-Bestimmungen stand danach nur noch das 1275er Triebwerk mit Benzin-Einspritzung zur Verfügung.

Natürlich kümmerte sich John Cooper nicht nur um die Entwicklung der schnellen Minis: er gehörte zu den Pionieren der Mittelmotor-Bauweise in der Formel 1, Jack Brabham wurde auf seinem Auto Weltmeister. Auch im Portfolio des New Mini lebt sein Name weiter. 2001 wurde der neue Cooper (und später der Cooper S) vorgestellt. Das John-Cooper-Works-Programm bietet auch heute noch vielen Mini-Fahrern die Möglichkeit, ihr Auto individuell zu veredeln. Das geht von Leistungssteigerungen bis auf mehr als 200 PS über optische Retuschen bis hin zum Sondermodell „JCW GP". John Cooper selber erlebte die neue Generation „seines" Autos nicht mehr: er starb am 24. Dezember 2000. Sein Sohn Mike Cooper hat das Erbe sicherlich absolut würdig angetreten und sorgt dafür, dass der Familienname auch weiterhin mit dem Mini verbunden wird.

3. MUCH MORE THAN A CAR

Bald ein halbes Jahrhundert ist es her, dass der Mini erstmals präsentiert wurde. Welche Popularität der Kleine aus Longbridge im Laufe der Zeit erlangen sollte, konnte damals wohl niemand ahnen. Eigentlich war das Auto ja eher unter nüchternen ökonomischen Aspekten als familiengerechter Kleinwagen entwickelt worden. Bedingt durch das einzigartige Design, sein faszinierendes technisches Konzept sowie sportliche Erfolge avancierte der Mini jedoch im Laufe der Zeit zum absoluten Kultfahrzeug. Doch damit nicht genug. In beispielsloser Weise wurde die Neuinterpretation des seit 2000 nicht mehr gebauten ursprünglichen Mini umgehend zu einer Lifestyle-Ikone der Gegenwart.

Die Begeisterung für den Mini äußert sich in einer ausgeprägten Szene von Fans und Enthusiasten, die in vielfältiger Weise ihrer Begeisterung sowohl für das alte als auch das neue Auto nachgehen. Sei es, dass man sich der Restauration und dem Erhalt des Klassikers widmet, Tuning- oder Rennsport-begeistert ist oder ganz einfach den Reiz auskostet, Teil einer weltweiten Community zu sein. Seit eh und je existieren Mini-Clubs - längst nicht allein in Großbritannien, sondern in vielen weiteren Ländern der Erde. Darüber hinaus gibt es spezielle Rennserien sowie teilweise groß angelegte Treffen. Zu den einschlägigen Events gehören unter anderem die internationalen Meetings der Mini-Classic-Fans an wechselnden Standorten. Dazu gibt es Veranstaltungen wie „Strahlung pur", die „Hamburg Mini Days" und die „Braunschweiger Mini Tage" in Deutschland, „Mini Mania" in England, „Mini Mucchio" in Italien oder „Mini takes the States" in den USA. Besonders zu erwähnen ist, dass die Mini-Community über privates und werksunabhängiges Engagement hinaus in besonderer Weise auch durch die Bayerischen Motorenwerke gefördert wird. Das bisher größte Event dieser Art ist „Mini United", das 2005 im italienischen Misano Premiere feierte. Gleich beim ersten Mal kamen rund 6000 Mini-Fans aus 40 Staaten mit über 4000 Autos an die Adria-

Küste. Im Juni 2007 gab es ein weiteres Treffen, wobei die Nordsee die Kulisse der Mega-Veranstaltung bieten sollte. Im „Circuit Park" des niederländischen Zandvoort konnten die Organisatoren dabei mit 8000 Besuchern einen noch deutlichen Zuwachs gegenüber des schon äußerst beachtenswerten ersten Meeting verzeichnen. Von daher bleibt mit Spannung abzuwarten, wie sich „Mini United" weiterentwickeln wird...

4. ALWAYS A RACER

Keine Frage, bei seiner Premiere 1959 war der Mini eine Sensation – und da Automobilhersteller ihre Kompetenz gerne im Motorsport unter Beweis stellen, schickte BMC ihn auf die Piste. Ein halbes Jahr nach der Markteinführung starteten sechs Werkswagen zur Rallye Monte Carlo. Die gleiche Anzahl an Minis wurde von Privatfahrern an den Start gestellt. Das Team Riley/Jones fuhr das beste Resultat ein: einen ernüchternden 23. Platz.

Im Jahr 1961 sah keiner der drei gestarteten Werkswagen das Ziel. Hinter den Kulissen wurde getüftelt und getestet. 1962 startete man abermals bei der Rallye Monte Carlo. Der Finne Rauno Aaltonen sollte für BMC die Kohlen aus dem Feuer holen. Doch nach einem Überschlag brannte sein Auto aus. Die verbleibenden Werks-Minis landeten auf den Plätzen 26 und 77. BMC beobachtete auch das übrige Feld: Privatfahrer Timo Mäkinen schlug sich in seinem Cooper nicht schlecht; auch der Ire Patrick Hopkirk im Sunbeam Rapier wurde argwöhnisch beäugt. Ein Jahr später saß er in einem von vier Werks-Minis. Er wurde hinter seinem Teamkollegen Aaltonen Klassenzweiter, im Gesamtklassement belegte der Finne den dritten, der Ire den sechsten Platz. Die Rallye-Welt horchte auf: Da fuhren doch zwei Kleinwagen den „Großen" regelrecht um die Ohren!

Der Durchbruch gelang 1964: sechs Werks- und 24 private Minis traten gegen die vermeintlich starke Konkurrenz an. Der Rest ist Legende: Paddy Hopkirk gewinnt die Rallye Monte Carlo. Auf Rang Vier folgt mit Timo Mäkinen der nächste Mini-Fahrer, Aaltonen wird Gesamtsiebter. Die Sensation ist perfekt!

Erfolg verpflichtet: Die Rallye Monte Carlo 1965 galt im Nachhinein neben der 52er Veranstaltung als bisher härteste Prüfung von Mensch und Material. Eis und Schnee trennten die Spreu vom Weizen. 35 von 237 gestarteten Autos sahen das Ziel! Unter den wenigen, die durchgehalten haben, waren gleich drei Minis. Und in einem solchen hatten Timo Mäkinen/Christobel Carlisle die Gesamtwertung gewonnen!

Im Jahr 1966 vereitelte eine umstrittene Entscheidung der Sportkommissare den Hattrick bei der „Monte Carlo". Mäkinen, Aaltonen und Hopkirk sausten dem Feld um die Ohren. Doch bei der technischen Abnahme entschied man, dass die Zusatzscheinwerfer vor dem Kühler nicht den französischen Zulassungsbestimmungen entsprächen.

1968 beschloss BMC-Chef Lord Stokes die Auflösung der Motorsport-Abteilung, ein letztes Mal sollte die wilde Meute den Col de Turini erklimmen. Mit den Plätzen drei, vier und fünf (Aaltonen, Fall, Hopkirk) verabschiedeten sich die mittlerweile legendären Autos von der Piste. Doch sowohl der Mini wie auch seine damaligen Fahrer sind immer wieder auf allen Rennstrecken dieser Welt zu finden - bei Oldtimerrennen wie der British Car Trophy in Deutschland, bei Rallyes und Gleichmäßigkeits-Prüfungen. Zahllose Privatteams schätzen die Qualitäten des Classics noch heute.

Auch der New Mini wird zum beliebten Renngerät: in der von Mike Cooper initiierten John-Cooper-Challenge starteten 2002 erstmals alte Hasen ebenso wie heißblütige Youngster. Aufgrund der großen Resonanz wurden nach und nach nationale Meisterschaften (auch unter dem Namen „Mini Challenge") etabliert. In Misano fuhr man 2005 erstmals ein Weltfinale aus, dass der Belgier Maxime Martin für sich entscheiden konnte.

Immer wieder setzen sich prominente Gaststarter in die über 200 PS starken Autos. Die Fahrer genießen das kartmäßige Handling des JCW-Cooper S, die Zuschauer erfreuen sich an den spannenden Fights auf der Strecke, wenn bis zu vierzig gleichwertige Autos um die Platzierungen kämpfen. Der Mini und der Motorsport - es gehört einfach zusammen!

5. VARIETIES AND FANTASIES

Seit eh und je regt der Mini die Fantasien an. Nicht nur die seiner Fans, die ihn zuweilen nach Herzenslust modifizieren, sondern auch der Konstrukteure und Werksdesigner. Vor allem, um zusätzliche Käufergruppen zu erschließen, entstanden über die Jahre hinweg verschiedene Fahrzeugtypen auf Basis des kleinen Briten. Die ein oder andere dieser Varianten dürfte der mit der Modellgeschichte weniger Vertraute vielleicht gar nicht mal auf Anhieb dem Mini-Lager zuordnen. Das wohl mit markanteste Beispiel: der ursprünglich als Militärfahrzeug vorgesehene offene Moke. Bei dem „Lasttier" hatte man anfangs gar mit zwei Motoren in einem Auto experimentiert. Vorn ein 950-ccm-Aggregat und im Heck der 850er Serienmotor sollten dem im wesentlichen auf dem Mini Countryman basierenden Winzling einen geländetauglichen Allradantrieb bescheren. Erste Prototypentests zeigten allerdings schon bald, dass der Moke keinesfalls mit einem Jeep oder Land Rover konkurrieren konnte. Es gab vor allem Probleme mit der Kühlung sowie der Synchronisation der beiden Treibsätze. Dennoch versuchte man es zunächst noch mit einer Kombination von zwei Triebwerken aus dem Austin 1100, bevor das „Twin-Mini"-Konzept endgültig fallen gelassen wurde. Nach einigem Hin und Her kam der Moke schließlich als Freizeitfahrzeug mit 850-ccm-Standardmotorisierung samt Frontantrieb auf den zivilen Markt. Allemal genug für eine Spritztour ins Grüne oder die Fahrt zum Strand. Bei der angepeilten eher wohlhabenden Zielgruppe wurde das Auto schließlich regelrecht zum Trendgefährt.

So fernab des ursprünglichen Mini fallen andere Varianten allerdings nicht unbedingt aus. So zeigen die heute Kultstatus genießenden Pick-Up-Modelle weitaus deutlicher ihre Herkunft, während die Clubmans wiederum durch eine eigentlich gar nicht Mini-typische Front auffallen. Egal ob man nun die noblen Wolseleys, das schicke Cabrio, den Countryman, den als Transporter konzipierten Mini-Van oder Estate nimmt, Vielfältigkeit ist beim Mini immer ein bedeutsames Thema gewesen. Vom Werk nicht angebotenen Ausführungen haben sich gerne auch externe Anbieter angenommen. Man denke beispielsweise nur an die sportlichen Midas auf Mini-Basis oder den Nomad, einen Umbau im Land-Rover-Look von einem britischen Hersteller. Und alles was der Fantasie rund um die automobilen Winzlinge sonst noch entspringen kann, stellen engagierte Schrauber und eingefleischte Mini-Enthusiasten ohnehin nur allzugerne komplett selbst auf die Räder. Das Spektrum reicht dabei vom Big Foot über andere Fun-Cars bis hin zur Stretchlimousine.

6. THE LEGEND LIVES!

Der Mini ist für unzählige seiner Besitzer fraglos weitaus mehr als etwas, womit man von A nach B kommen kann. Aber trotz aller Emotionalität wurde der kleine Brite letztendlich doch von rein rationalen Entscheidungen eingeholt. Über vier Jahrzehnte nahezu unverändert gebaut, ist die Produktion des altvertrauten Mini im Jahr 2000 eingestellt worden. Umgehend ging jedoch ein Nachfolger in Form einer von BMW auf den Markt gebrachten Neuinterpretation an den Start.
Bei der Entwicklung des Mini für das neue Jahrtausend hatte längst nicht allein der Retrogedanke Pate gestanden, vielmehr verkörpert der im September 2000 in Paris vorgestellte New Mini die Evolution des Originals. Die Gemeinsamkeiten mit dem Vorgänger beschränkten sich dabei auf den Namen und die Grundform. Wobei das wie der klassische Mini in England gebaute neue Auto zunächst nur als Einstiegsversion One und als sportlicher Cooper angeboten wurde. Jeweils von einem 1,6 Liter-Vierzylinder mit 90 bzw. 115 PS getrieben, sollten aber schnell weitere Motor- und Modellvarianten inclusive Cabrio folgen. 2006 ging dann darüber hinaus bereits der Neue unter den Neuen an den Start, denn BMW hatte zum Jahresende den ersten Generationswechsel beim New Mini eingeleitet. Ein deutlicheres Zeichen, dass sich der Nachfolger des klassischen Mini allen anfänglichen Unkenrufen zum Trotz bewährt hatte, konnte es wohl kaum geben.

Besagte Evolution des Originals fortzuführen, verpflichtet in besonderer Weise. So war man – wie kaum anders zu erwarten – im Bezug auf äußere Modifikationen mit sehr viel Feingefühl vorgegangen. Auf den ersten Blick sieht der New Mini II, obwohl jedes einzelne Blechteil anders geformt wurde, gar nicht so neu aus. Beim näheren Hinsehen offenbart er jedoch einiges an optischen Änderungen: Mit der ein Stück in die Höhe gewachsenen Motorhaube wirkt der Zweier etwas bulliger, das Heck ist markanter gestylt, und es werden wohl noch ein wenig mehr sportliche Assoziationen als schon beim Vorgänger freigesetzt. Ebenfalls komplett überarbeitet zeigt sich das Interieur mit dem äußerst markanten, überdimensionalen Center-Speedo. Und was die Technik angeht, haben die jüngsten Modelle die Bezeichnung „neu" ohnehin im wahrsten Sinne des Wortes verdient. Allem voran sind die mit dem Generationswechsel eingeführten beiden neuen Motoren aufzuführen. Vor der Wachablösung des One im Jahr 2007 sowie der weiteren Ausweitung der Modellpalette präsentierte man zum Start in die zweite Runde zunächst einen Cooper sowie Cooper S. Das 175 PS starke 1,6-Liter-Triebwerk von letzterem wird mittels eines Twin-Scroll-Turbos aufgeladen, während dem Basis-Cooper ein 120-PS-Sauger mit BMW-Valvetronic Beine macht. Nicht unerwähnt darf bleiben, dass der im Vergleich mit der Urausführung ohnehin schon nicht mehr wirklich kleine Mini noch einmal um sechs Zentimeter gewachsen ist.
Auf alle Fälle aber gehören dem New Mini längst die Herzen einer beeindruckend großen und stetig wachsenden Anhängerschaft. Denn der aktuelle Mini hat eindeutig bewiesen, dass er analog zu seinem Vorgänger über den Nutzwert hinaus das Zeug hat, in höchster Weise auch auf emotionaler Ebene anzusprechen. Es besteht kein Zweifel: Die Legende lebt!

7. THE LATEST STEP

Jede Modellreihe im Automobilbau lebt von der Veränderung, das ist beim New Mini nicht anders als bei seinem Vorbild. Immer wieder gab es neue Varianten. So war es nur eine Frage der Zeit, bis ein neuer „Estate" in die Showrooms der Händler rollte. Aber von der ersten Skizze bis zum Serienmodell ist es ein langer Weg. Das Designteam um Gerd Hildebrand stellte auf den Automessen 2005/6 vier Beispiele vor, wie ein künftiger "Traveller" - so der frühere Name des Kombis - aussehen könnte.
Auf der IAA Frankfurt stand die Reiselust im Vordergrund. Eine flexible, herausziehbare Cargobox wird sichtbar, wenn man die hinteren Türen öffnet. Weißes Leder, Chrom und Aluminium laden zum Platznehmen und Losfahren ein. Kleiner Gag am Rande: Die Cup-Holder sind direkt vor den Luftausströmern montiert. So werden Erfrischungsgetränke im Sommer von der Klimaanlage gekühlt, im Winter hält die Heizung Tee oder Kaffee warm.
„Go British" war das Motto in Tokio. Das changierende „Satellite Silver" erhielt neue Akzente in Grün und Messing-Optik. Das erinnert an das klassische „British Racing Green" englischer Rennwagen. Die Messingapplikationen spiegeln das Flair Londoner Clubs wieder. Anstelle der Seitenfenster wurden Picknickboxen integriert. Eine herausnehmbare Scheibe im Dach dient bei Bedarf als Tisch. Die Sports Utility Box nimmt auf, was sonst noch zu einem gelungenen Nachmittag gehört – die Cricket- oder Tennisausrüstung beispielsweise.
„Go Sports!", hieß es in Detroit, wo die Serienfertigung des Travellers verkündet wurde. Das Concept präsentierte sich raubeinig wie ein typisch amerikanischer SUV. Zuhause werden die Sportgeräte in das auswechselbare Staufach gepackt, das sich vor der Fahrt schnell einhängen lässt. Dank der Klappe über den Hecktüren kann man sogar ein Surfbrett mitnehmen! Auf der Reling des "Concept Detroit" lassen sich die Querträger verschieben. Wenn gar nichts mehr geht, kann der Mini mit einer Dachbox versehen werden. Rote und blaue Elemente oder die Streifen auf der Motorhaube tragen den „Stars & Stripes" des Gastgeberlandes Rechnung.
In Genf präsentierte Mini 2006 die vierte Variante. Dieses Mal erinnerte man an den legendären Sieg bei der Rallye Monte Carlo 1964. Die Sports Utility Box wird zur Werkzeugkiste: alles, was Fahrer und Beifahrer unterwegs brauchen, sitzt an seinem

Platz, die Cargobox bietet Stauraum für Ersatzteile. Ein markantes Merkmal von Rallye-Fahrzeugen ist das Reserverad in Griffnähe. „Concept Geneva" bietet eine eigene Mulde im Dachbereich, aus der das fünfte Rad mit zwei Bügelgriffen heruntergeholt werden kann. „Typisch Rallye" sind die Zusatzleuchten im Grill. Klar, dass diese Studie nur rot-weiß werden konnte – diese Farbkombination ist spätestens seit dem 24. Januar 1964 Kult unter Mini-Fahrern!

Die Studien testeten die Resonanz des Publikums. Welches Gimmick sollte erhalten bleiben, was ist überflüssig? Auf der Internationalen Automobil Ausstellung 2007 in Frankfurt präsentierte Mini dann das Serienmodell, den Clubman. Geblieben sind auf jeden Fall die markanten, weit öffnenden Türen am Heck. So könnte dem Kombi auch ein Kastenwagen zur Seite gestellt werden: mit geschlossenen Seitenteilen wäre er sicher ein willkommener Sympathieträger für Kurierdienste und Handwerksbetriebe…

8. MINI MUSIC – THE BEAT GOES ON…

So außergewöhnlich die Idee eines earBOOKs zum Thema Mini auch erscheinen mag, so naheliegend war sie. Denn nichts könnte unser Portfolio aus Bildern und Zeitdokumenten besser ergänzen als eine Sammlung von Musikstücken aus den Jahren, in denen der Mini zum wahren Kultauto wurde, obwohl er eigentlich ja eher ein aus rein rationalen Erwägungen konzipierter Kleinwagen war. Die aus vier CDs bestehende Kollektion mit über 40 Titeln ist sozusagen der Soundtrack einer Erfolgsgeschichte. Auf der anderen Seite aber auch ganz einfach Musik, die den Spaß am Mini noch weiter beflügeln kann. Eine derartige Compilation musste zwangsläufig so facettenreich ausfallen, wie sich auch der Mini schon bald nach seiner Markteinführung zeigte. Deshalb ist alles dabei: Vom ungeschliffenen Beat aus den Anfangstagen des Winzling über verschiedenes aus dem Pop-Bereich bis hin zum schillernden Glam Rock, der den Mini auf seinem Weg als automobiler Star begleitete.

Es steht außer Frage: Mini und Musik gehören seit je her zusammen. Nicht zuletzt schon dadurch, dass nicht wenige Künstler den Kleinen selbst fahren oder fuhren beziehungsweise sich von ihm inspirieren ließen. Cliff Richard hatte einen Mini und auch jeder einzelne Beatle. Marc Bolan von T. Rex starb gar trauriger Weise bei einem Unfall in einem Clubman 1275 GT. Spencer Davis soll auf einer nächtlichen Überlandfahrt mit einem Mini, bei der das Benzin auszugehen drohte, der Welthit „Keep on Running" in den Sinn gekommen sein. David Bowie gehörte zu den Prominenten, die anlässlich einer Aktion zum 40-jährigen Mini-Jubiläum 1999 ihre ganz persönliche Variante gestalteten. Das Ergebnis dabei: ein komplett chromglänzendes Exemplar! Von Herstellerseite wurden Mini und Musik schon ursprünglich gerne zusammengebracht, was auch unter neuer Flagge seine Fortsetzung findet. Während beispielsweise seinerzeit im Sondermodell Red Hot beim Kauf ein Walkman und eine Soul- und Chart-Hit-Cassette lagen, engagierte man 2006 Boy George als DJ für Mini's Urban Style Tour. Und mit „Def Mini Records" wurde jüngst gar ein Label ins Leben gerufen, das Bands wie „The Disc Brakes", „Runflat" oder „N'Cap" präsentiert. Klar, das ist nur ein Werbegag – aber wie auch immer Mini und Musik zusammenfinden, es gibt keinen Zweifel: The Beat goes on…

ÜBER DIE AUTOREN

Michael Stein, geboren 1959, absolvierte nach dem Studium an der Ruhr-universität Bochum eine weiterführende Ausbildung zum Technischen Redakteur. Seiner Begeisterung für außergewöhnliche Fahrzeuge folgend, stieg er mit der Arbeit für die deutsche Ausgabe des schwedischen Magazin „Wheels" in den Journalismus ein. Mittlerweile ist Michael Stein seit bald 15 Jahren für verschiedene renommierte Motortitel aus der Vestischen Mediengruppe Welke (Herten/Deutschland) tätig. Während dieser Zeit entwickelte er sich zum exzellenten Kenner der europäischen Szene von Automobilenthusiasten und Tuning-Fans. Gleichzeitig ist er international auf vielen einschlägigen Fachmessen unterwegs oder folgt den Einladungen der Fahrzeug- und Zubehörindustrie zu Testfahrten und Produktpremieren. Als Chefredakteur von MINI SCENE INTERNATIONAL und zudem auch im Musikbereich regelmäßig journalistisch aktiv, bringt Michael Stein jede Menge Fachkompetenz zu den Themen dieses earBOOK mit.

Thomas Pfahl, geboren 1973, ist Automann mit Leib und Seele. Unweit der legendären deutschen Rennstrecke Nürburgring aufgewachsen, interessiert er sich schon seit frühester Kindheit für alles, was vier Räder hat. Dabei spielte der Motorsport, ob auf der Rundstrecke oder bei Rallyes, schon immer eine große Rolle. So folgte dem Abitur eine Lehre zum Kfz-Mechaniker. 1997 nahm Thomas Pfahl neben dem Schraubenschlüssel auch noch die Kamera in die Hand: nach dem Praktikum in einer Tageszeitungs-Redaktion begann er sein Volontariat bei der Vestischen Mediengruppe Welke. Hier wirkte er fortan an diversen Magazinen mit. Etliche Fahrzeuge aller Couleur – von ihren Besitzern liebevoll veredelt oder restauriert – rückt er Tag für Tag textlich und bildlich ins rechte Licht, besucht die Treffen der Szene, testet Neuentwicklungen und diskutiert mit ihren Designern und Konstrukteuren. Als Chef vom Dienst begleitet Thomas Pfahl MINI SCENE INTERNATIONAL seit der ersten Ausgabe, die im September 2005 erschienen ist.

TRACKLIST

CD 1

#	Title	Artist	Time	Credits
1	Wild Thing	The Troggs	02:36	C.Taylor/C.Taylor · EMI Blackwood Music Inc. (BMI)
2	Sha La La La Lee	Small Faces	02:49	Lynch/Shuman · Carlin Music Corp. · P 1966 Decca Music Group Ltd
3	Hippy Hippy Shake	Swinging Blue Jeans	02:03	Romero · Accord Musikverlag GmbH
4	I'm The One	Gerry & The Pacemakers	02:15	Marsden · Dick James Music Ltd
5	Do You Love Me	Brian Poole & The Tremeloes	02:25	B. Gordy Jr. · Jobete Music
6	Game Of Love	Wayne Fontana	02:04	Ballard · Skidmore Music Co. Inc.(ASCAP)
7	Happy Together	The Turtles	02:50	Bonner/Gordon · EMI Publishing
8	Hold Me	PJ Proby	02:41	Little/Oppenheim/Schuster · Campbell, Conelly & Co Ltd
9	Crimson And Clover	Tommy James	03:29	James/Lucio
10	Jesamine	The Casuals	03:37	Manston/Gellar · Bellwin Mills Music Ltd
11	Pied Piper	Crispian St. Peters	02:26	Kornfield/Duboff · David Nicolson/EMI
12	You Don't Have To Say You Love Me	Dusty Springfield	02:48	Donaggio/Pallavicini · B. Feldman & Co Ltd/EMI United Partnership Ltd · P 1966 Mercury Records Ltd
13	Tonight	The Rubettes	03:34	Bickerton/Waddington · MCA Music GmbH
14	When A Man Loves A Woman	Percy Sledge	02:56	Lewis/Wright · Pronto Music Inc./Quinvy Music Inc. (BMI)
15	Ferry Cross The Mersey	Gerry & The Pacemakers	02:27	Marsden · Universal/Dick James Music

CD 2

#	Title	Artist	Time	Credits
1	All Or Nothing	Small Faces	03:01	Marriott/Lane · Aquarius Music Ltd · P 1966 Decca Music Group Ltd
2	Land Of A Thousand Dances	The Walker Brothers	02:35	Domino/Kenner · Thursday Music Corp. · P 1965 Mercury Records Ltd
3	Silence Is Golden	The Tremeloes	03:14	Crewe/Gaudio · Saturday Music Inc./Gavadima Music (ASCAP)
4	Sugar Baby Love	The Rubettes	03:30	Bickerton/Waddington · ATV Music Ltd
5	Baby Come Back	The Equals	02:38	E. Grant · Hanseatic MV GmbH
6	You Were On My Mind	Crispian St Peters	02:43	Fricker · Witmark M & Sons (ASCAP)
7	Hitchin' A Ride	Vanity Fare	02:55	Callander/Murray · Universal-Polygram International Publishing Inc. (BMI)
8	Young Girl	Gary Puckett & The Union Gap	03:10	Fuller · Warner-Tamerlane Publishing Corp. (BMI)
9	Eloise	Barry Ryan	05:45	Ryan · Carlin Music Corp · P 1969 Universal Music Domestic Division, a divison of Universal Music GmbH
10	I'd Like To teach The World To Sing	New Seekers	02:31	Backer/Cook/Davis/Greenaway · Shada Music Inc. (ASCAP)
11	Tell It Like It Is	Percy Sledge	02:35	Davis/Diamond · Conrad Music/Orlap Publ.
12	Me And You And A Dog Named Boo	Lobo	03:11	La Voie · Famous Music Publishing Co. (ASCAP)
13	Flowers In The Rain	Carl Wayne	02:26	Wood · Westminster Music Ltd

CD 3

1	I Close My Eyes And Count To Ten	Dusty Springfield	03:10	Westlake · Carlin Music Corp · P 1968 Mercury Records Ltd
2	Fox On The Run	Manfred Mann	02:44	Hazzard · Mann Music Publ. Ltd · P 1968 Mercury Records Ltd
3	Rock Your Baby	George McCrae	03:20	Casey/Finch · Peer Southern
4	Dizzy	Tommy Roe	02:58	Roe/Weller · Low-Twi Music Inc. (BMI)
5	I'd Love You To Want Me	Lobo	04:11	La Voie · Famous Music Publishing Co. (ASCAP)
6	Love Is All Around	The Troggs	02:40	R. Presley/R. Presley · Dick James Music
7	You'll Never walk Alone	Gerry & The Pacemakers	02:26	Hammerstein/Rodgers · Williamson Music Inc. (ASCAP)
8	Hole In My Shoe	Traffic	03:04	Mason · Essex Music Inc. · P 1967 Universal Music Domestic Division, a divison of Universal Music GmbH
9	Let's Get Together Again	The Glitter Band	03:57	Rossall/Shephard · Filmtrax Plc
10	Juke Box Jive	The Rubettes	02:12	Bickerton/Waddington · MCA Music GmbH
11	Itsy Bitsy Teeny Weeny	ShaNaNa	02:26	Vance/Pockriss · Gobal Musikverlag
12	If I Had A Hammer	Trini Lopez	02:56	Hayes/Seeger · TRO-Ludlow Music, Inc. (BMI)
13	Rama Lama Ding Dong	ShaNaNa	02:23	G. Jones Jr · Multitune Inc.
14	Sweets For My Sweet	The Drifters	02:40	Pomus/Shuman · Trio Music Co. Inc./Hill & Range Songs (BMI)

CD 4

1	Hold Tight	Dave Dee, Dozy, Beaky, Mick & Tich	02:46	Tudor Blaikley/Howard · Lynn Music Ltd · P 1966 Mercury Records Ltd
2	In The Summertime	Mungo Jerry	03:40	Dorset · Sony/ATV Songs LLC
3	In Zaire	Johnny Wakelin	03:30	Wakelin · Francis Day & Hunter Ltd
4	Hanky Panky	Tommy James	03:02	Barry/Greenwich · TM Music Ltd
5	Cry Like A Baby	The Box Tops	02:33	Penn/Oldham/Spooner · EMI Music Publishing
6	I Think Of You	The Merseybeats	02:23	P.L. Sterling
7	Come And Get It	Badfinger	02:21	Mc Cartney · ATV Music Corp. (ASCAP)
8	The Sun Ain't Gonna Shine Anymore	The Walker Brothers	03:03	Crewe/Gaudio · EMI Longitude Music Co./Seasons Four Music · P 1966 The Island Def Jam Music Group
9	Soul Man	Sam & Dave	02:38	Hayes/Porter · Almo Music Corp./Walden Music (ASCAP)
10	With A Girl Like You	The Troggs	02:15	R. Presley/R.Presley · Dick James Music
11	We've Only Just Begun	Lynn Anderson	03:16	Williams/Nichols · Rondor Music Ltd
12	Groovy Kind Of Love	Wayne Fontana	03.20	Wine/Bayer · Screen Gems/EMI Music
13	Raindrops	Dee Clark	02 :47	Clark · Conrad Music (BMI)
14	Angel Face	The Glitter Band	02:58	Rossall/Shephard · Filmtrax Plc
15	The Letter	The Box Tops	01:57	Thompson · Budde Songs Inc (BMI)